BROKEN PEOPLE

RACHEL THOMPSON

Contents

Water

Acknowlegements

It's finally here, in your hands. Book Three in my *Broken Series*. And it wouldn't be without the help of my amazingly patient and brilliant editor, Cristina Houghton Lawrence, who finishes my sentences when we talk, like a sister, which she is. A survivor sister. Which she is. We are kindred.

To the ever-patient Barb Drozdowich, who knows everything about everything bookish.

To my survivor sisters, Judith Staff, who reads my work and continues to remind me when I'm feeling overwhelmed this writing gig is worth it, and who is teaching me how to accept compliments because I'm shit at it; Dr. Alexandria Szeman, who, despite massive hardships, impresses me daily with her kindness and support; and Melissa Flickinger who runs circles around me and keeps me on track, somehow. I'm forever grateful to my girls.

Mom and Dad, Caren and Chris, Leslie and Bryce and fam, Sarah and Chris and fam – love you all.

As always, much love to my children, Anya and Lukas, who are constant sources of inspiration and who continue to motivate me to help make this a better world, if only in my own, tiny way. Our house rules are 1) Be respectful and 2) Clean up your shit. None of us is perfect, yet, imagine if everyone in the world did the same.

And most importantly, to J. He knows why.

Introduction

How do I write my books? Every writer is different. I'm a combo plotter/pantser. I think of a word or theme, noodle it around my brain for a day or a week, journal about it, maybe even blog about it. I will most likely research it a bit as well (the journalist in me). Then, without an outline, off I go. No self-editing, no stopping, I ignore everything in real life and just *go*. Into the flow.

Doesn't matter if what I write is terrible (and yes, it can be and that's okay!), I simply keep writing until there is, eventually, enough to go back over and try to make some sense out of. And that's what I love about the creative process: from this mess, patterns emerge.

And that's exactly what happened with this book. The elements appeared – fire, air, earth, water. We're at their mercy one way or another, whether we realize or believe (just watch The Weather Channel sometime). Simply being alive is dependent on the air we breathe and the water we drink. As Maslow figured out ages ago, we tend to our basic needs first. How can we heal if we don't have those needs under control?

As for the title *Broken People*, it fits with my overall theme. Do I believe I'm broken? Do I believe all sexual abuse and rape survivors are *broken*? In some ways, yes. Anyone who has lived through severe trauma can't help but be affected, even on a cellular, subconscious level, as I discuss in my previous books.

I also believe we can grow from those challenges. We have the capacity to heal. We each have a journey to repair the ways in which perpetrators of the crimes against us not only stole our innocence but in many ways, broke it. We'll never regain that innocence. It's gone forever.

We can, however, find joy.
We did nothing wrong.
We deserve love and support.

Make that your mantra.

Foreword

Having followed Rachel for a while on Twitter, I messaged her one afternoon, years ago. I had seen something on her #SexAbuseChat hashtag and wanted to comment but couldn't. When I messaged her privately, still I could not get the words out. It didn't matter - she knew what they were, anyway, and responded to me with all the kindness and warmth I needed in that moment, despite being an ocean away.

Rachel speaks for survivors of sexual abuse in the most succinct and deeply articulate of ways. She gets it, she gets us, and she has our backs. As if that is not formidable enough, she also has a tremendous capacity to communicate to those on the outside, too. Those who do not understand, those who are supporting survivors as loved ones, or those wishing to fight with survivors, starting battles we are too tired to enter.

Rachel always finds the words, hoping in her own way, to close the sometimes-vast gap of understanding between those on both sides of the sexual abuse wall which divides us – the survivors and the never-abused. Endlessly striving to help survivors feel seen and heard, she makes sure her door is always open – fielding messages, and sharing her writing widely, always there for those moments of ice-cold isolation.

Aware of the pivotal role of non-survivors in the journey of heal-ing, Rachel gently and firmly guides them in seeking the best way to hold space for their loved ones. She shows an incredible empathy and knows first-hand the deep-seated benefits for them of developing their understanding so they can grow their relationship while supporting the survivor on her or his journey of healing.

This third book in her Broken series, *Broken People* is both heart wrenching in its honesty, and hope-filled in its commitment to recov-ery. Through her beautiful, gently scribed work, Rachel shows the destruction that sexual abuse causes, and also the hope and strength that is conceived in the healing process. She speaks to you, the reader, like a warm friend who is by your side. For survivors, Rachel's voice is that of a wise older sister, looking out for you and comforting you when you feel alone with all the carnage that sexual trauma can leave in its wake.

I am truly honoured to know Rachel in person and can promise you that her authentic self is in every ink-soaked page of this book. By giving so generously of her spirit, and her understanding, while intent on making a human connection with every reader, Rachel has succeeded, yet again, in creating a book which speaks to the hurt parts inside some of us, and the empathetic parts in those around us.

Finally, if you have not yet read the first two books, *Broken Pieces* and *Broken Places*, you might just want to after reading this beautiful gem.

~ Judith Staff, Post Graduate Certificate in Education, Post Graduate Diploma in Integrated Provision for Early Years, United Kingdom
https://judithstaffmusings.com/

My name is Dr. Shruti Kapoor. I am a survivor of child sexual abuse. Together, Rachel and I started Speak Our Stories, a platform for survivors to share their stories of sexual abuse and journey of healing.

When Rachel asked me to write the forward for *Broken People*, I was beyond honored. I connected with this book in more ways than words can explain. As survivors of sexual abuse, we all go through unique journeys and experiences. In *Broken People*, Rachel shares her challenges, the process of recovery, and what healing has looked like for her over the years.

Unfortunately, we all live in a society that puts the onus of women and girls' safety on them. If we get into trouble, have been sexually violated, we must have done something wrong. Women and girls are made to believe they are at fault for the abuse they experience. Survivors carry the burden and shame of their abuse for decades, thereby impacting themselves physically, mentally, and in more ways one can imagine.

In *Broken People*, Rachel Thompson shares the impact and aftermath of the sexual abuse she faced as a little girl. She carried guilt and shame, was forced to live right next to her abuser for many years, experienced depression, PTSD and many other socio-psychological challenges. She talks about the challenges of raising a family, of being in romantic relationships, and as a parent.

While reading through Rachel's story, I found myself crying, getting angry, feeling pain, sympathy, frustration, and love for her. Anger at the abuser for having violated the space of a little innocent girl, frustration at the laws and our society for forcing her to live right next to her abuser, and experiencing more pain and fear. Sympathy for the little girl who felt shame and carried the guilt for many years of her life, and love for the woman who despite the challenges, has emerged as an empowered person helping herself, her family, and millions of other women through her work and advocacy.

Broken People is a book of courage, resilience and overcoming challenges Rachel faced as a survivor. Through her three books *Pieces, Places and Broken People*, Rachel has courageously shared her truth and the journey of her life. It's not all rosy and pretty and that's the beauty of these books. They represent the truth of a survivor, a mother, an empowered person who was made to believe she has no charge in her life but challenged that, and emerged on the other side.

These books have not only allowed her to openly share her experiences, they also provide hope, guidance, and a way forward for girls and women who feel they have no hope left in them.

Someone I trusted sexually abused me as a little girl. For three decades I carried the guilt and shame, keeping it all a secret in my heart. I felt confused, ashamed, and angry for what happened to me, but I never could muster the courage to share my story. Strong women like Rachel have given me the courage to today openly talk about my abuse. Your story matters, our stories matter. You never know how it might help someone.

Thank You, Rachel, for having the courage, conviction and resilience to share your truth with the world. Through this book and others, I hope survivors all over will find a way to move ahead and build the best life for themselves.

~ Dr. Shruti Kapoor
    Founder, Sayfty Trust

Fire

Fools

It bothered him.

I had secrets he knew about, and even more he didn't.

He wasn't the one,
after all those many years,
I felt like giving my secrets' virginity to,
scorching his ego more than how I secretly laughed at—and
loathed—
his thirty-second erections.

I am the fool because I stay.
It is enough.

Treating me that way,
the only way he knows but doesn't see,
twisting his thorny truths to fit flat in his palm of lies.

I am the fool because he stays.
He is enough.

No, I don't want to listen anymore!
I can't hear what will happen—what might change—
meaningless letters dripping from his tongue, digging into my skin.

Decades of faith lost inside my bones—
I gasp at the sharp, messy realization of my mistake.

I loved him.
Something so simple becomes so terribly complicated.
I believed in him,
and then I didn't.

Left to right, right to left,
up and down, down and up,
marching marching marching through endless days.
Opposites attract until they collide and atoms smash,
leaving behind an explosive mess of ashes and pain.

But we didn't explode.
It was more a quiet implosive retreat,
patiently gathering my forces and wits,
strategically placing every moment on my hidden board of fools,
waiting, biding, holding each breath,
pushing down every bitter verbal volley until I could finally, finally
say it:
Leave.

I don't want your noise
your clutter
your patronizing cuts
your condescension
your hands that touch me without feeling
your eyes that don't see
your ears that don't hear
your mouth that interrupts
your arms that don't fold me in
your lies you believe

your lies you can't see
your lies you don't hear
your stories that have become so real to you
you don't even realize they never happened
your lies
your lies
your lies.

These were the secrets I held, and still hold,
not for him, not against him, not because of him.
No matter how long we are with one partner,
we still have a secret inner life,
desires that sustain us,
folded up like paper hearts hidden in the deepest pockets of our
souls.
We fear the unfolding for what it will show,
the razing it may cause,
the cozy veneer of lies it burns away.

Fooling myself no longer.

I am enough.

Elements on Fire

It's all in the ending, regardless of how it begins, causing water to steam, fire to crackle, earth to heat, air to move. The elements are angry, my worry stones tell me, as I roll them across my aching fingers, biting at my bones. Heavy bones, tired of the weight I carry, this burden of a love I'm supposed to feel, one that is written and raised, sun pinging off a peeling golden seal, perfunctorily created in some airy office in California by an hourly clerk I've never met. Intimacy marked by agency, diametrically opposed.

What a strange little dance we've created, this business of love, that which started from binding twine or ribbon to one-upmanship in millions of dollars in flowers that die, of clear, shiny rocks pulled out of caves on the backs of babies, of twinkly lights that carry no meaning. Yet, if every intimacy of marriage is different, how is it that the human condition of energy and fluid exchange is no different? The song remains the same.

My body moves me forward because that's where I'm supposed to be. I can't go back to that silent place of quiet fury and prickly doubt, feeling my worry stones compelling me to go, move, jump, girl! Taking responsibility, blaming myself, for not creating enough crackling fire or earthy warmth, yet in the end it wasn't about that, really.

It's not about me, or him, or us. It's not about shedding the skins of blame or dusting the detritus of what little clarity remains. It's about the energy surrounding us, undulating in circular waves and unseen, infinite patterns.

It's a lie that all the elements work together in unison—they fight for prominence, just as we fight for the one we need, filling our core, giving us life.

I needed air to move.

To end.

To begin.

Just Fine

I'm not who you want me to be and that's *fine*.

No, it's not fine.
Fine is fucked. Fuck you, fine.
Fine means cool, copacetic, mellow.
You think that's what it means to be me.

I am hot,
I am *not* in excellent order,
I am tired
of you telling me what to do
how to feel
what to think
how to be.
I am not your mother's daughter.
I am me.

I brazenly sashay my swinging hips
up to your delicious mouth
dripping with their coarse demands …
chewing your thick, cherry lips,

tearing your lost mumblings
as red drips from my gnashing teeth.
Who owns your wants now?

This tough girl who used to quietly shrink at your words,
my heart shoves hard at my chest, wanting out.
Tears form and fall as I wipe them away with a furious fist.
Hating to admit how much it hurts
when you shred me.

Why do you think what you say matters?

Stunning, how the breeze flows without your say.
Pebbles may move in your wake,
but never trees.

I, Prey

She wants, just once, to shake this feeling men want her as only a sexual being. At the end of a day just south of bearable, as she finally lies down, sinking into her man won't be about touching that leads to something else.

Can't it be about touching for touching's sake? Affection and appreciation apparently not on the agenda she wants, and fails, to assert. When did what her lover wants now become her cross to bear?

Damned either way, her body cries …

Why is it always about sex?

A caged animal slipping, exposed, nowhere to go. So, she gives and receives and they, the various lovers of her heart, compliment her, tell her how sexy she is, how skilled. She barely hears their impassioned murmurs, her mind pushing down the groping squeezes and tantalizing strokes, smiling at them as she weaves a web in her mind to capture these sweet nothings to feast on later.

With the right person, she finds sex transcendent. It's not that she doesn't want it, crave it, find pleasure inside those wavy folds of bliss. Most lovers don't understand her intense need for affection—then again, they weren't used for sex as a child either.

She acknowledges this block, the way the memories exist in her mind like a prey's resistance, a gift her abuser so generously left behind.

"Now I lay me down to fuck," she whispers to her new lover.

He smiles, kissing her many scars, dark eyes paying them homage. Making different memories, she prays for acceptance. That she will not just get through it but allow him into her soul.

I Pray.

Velocity

The words rush by so quickly
not even sure I heard them
Mumbled in meanness,
garbled in glory,
taking the spoils of war
from our heavy chest of time.

I don't want any of it.
I've told you that for years.
The plates, the glasses, pristinely boxed and layered—
you placed it all gently so as not to break.
(Quite different from my heart.)

Drop the box
throw the glasses
rip the packing
shreds of who we were …
Shards cutting, blood rushing—
The velocity of love.

I Am Third-Person Past Tense

I am hyper-vigilant. I startle easily. Sometimes, I can't breathe.

When my skin would chill and I wanted to jump out of it, I'd scratch and tear and cry and hiccup and burst with newly birthed stars I couldn't understand or contain. I would listen to Pat Benatar over and over until I could count shaky breaths in rhythm to "I'm Gonna Follow You."

Breathe, dammit.

Focus, breathe.

Listen, breathe.

The words, the music, that voice soothing this wild child. Her ethereal, spectacular, operatic voice. I bet Benatar never imagined that inside the happy suburb of Fair Oaks, dark men lurked next door to damaged teen girls who just wanted to catch a deep breath, god fucking dammit.

I push through the panic, not even knowing it had a name. Hormones, episodes, teen-girl angst—that's what people around me called them. Overly sensitive. That's a good one. Nobody thinks to objectively attach repeated sexual abuse to panic attacks. As if the panic attacks were the issue.

Sometimes adults get things twisted.

I'm quiet. I watch people talk about me as if I'm not there. I am third-person past tense.

My thin, bony hands, the instruments of my future writing career—or piano, I haven't decided yet—hurt. They swell and ache. I ice them and take this new medicine called Advil. My worried folks think it's arthritis and take me for a bone scan.

I am fourteen. It is not arthritis.

"I can't breathe," I tell my mom.

She has me tested for asthma. My lungs are fine. Strong and clear, the lungs of an athlete, which I am. An elite gymnast, which I am. Until the coach's hand lingers too long on my backside, and I freeze. I tell my mom I don't want to go anymore.

"Why?" she asks.

"The girls are mean," I mumble, the best I can articulate.

She's glad. It was a far drive and cost a lot of money.

I still can't breathe.

The doctor suggests it's psychosomatic. That perhaps it's inflammation caused by stress. My mother suggests he kindly fuck off. There's nothing wrong with *her* straight-A-getting, never-in-trouble daughter. He advises she take me to a shrink.

She took me home to "Hit Me with Your Best Shot."

Smoke

I've lost ...
the desire to see you crumble
The wish to see you drown
The hope to see you struck down in the street
By a bolt of lightning
Or a car whipping out of nowhere

I've let you go.

I no longer ...
Gather tiny sparks of hate
In a glass jar tinted black with my fury
Kept high upon a shelf
To remind me of the whys
It's there if I need it

To let you go.

Now I ...
Breathe in the cool, fresh air
Of new love, of new life!

This dawning splendor
Combusting with heat around me
While you suffocate with rage

It's how you go.

I revel …
In my freedom
Without rancor
In what *I've* created
This future you don't belong in
This luminous life blazing with warmth.

You're gone.

Air

Unknowing

There are certain words survivors can't ever seem to escape:

"He said, she said."

"There's her side, his side, and the truth."

"She's just in it for the fame and money. Nothing really happened."

"She* put herself in that situation. She should have known better."

How many times must we read these persistent, blame-filled statements which dismiss, minimize, and assign fault to victims of sexual assault and rape? The language here puts all the emphasis and responsibility on the victim instead of the criminal who perpetrated the crimes.

This one, however, might be the worst:

"Why did she wait so long to report? It must not be true."

How does one equal the other? Many victims choose not to come forward out of shame, fear, reputation, power, loss of relationships with loved ones ... any number of reasons.

Sexual crimes are so incredibly invasive—people love to tell us *what they would have done*, yet they cannot imagine what it's like to live with these memories and triggers daily—memories of someone sexually invading you. Imagine what that's like. You probably can't. Which is why many people make these ridiculous statements.

The truth is, there are very real reasons why survivors don't report crimes that've happened to them. Here are just a few.

Self-Blame

Many survivors feel complicit—we blame ourselves. How could we put ourselves in a situation to be assaulted? How could we "let" it happen? Self-blame is rampant among sexual assault victims, made worse by others blaming and shaming us.

Sex complicates things. It's an intimate act. For an outsider, if sex is involved, they make assumptions:

- *How do we know she didn't want it?*
- *How do we know she didn't truly consent?*
- *How do we know she isn't lying?*
- *How do we know she doesn't have ulterior motives?*

In actuality, sexual assault and rape aren't about intimacy; they're about violence, control, and power. Invasion. Criminal acts. We *are* discussing crimes. Why is the victim required to prove their innocence?

For the victim whose entire life is now changed forever, these questions are not only invalidating as well as presumptuous, but they're also almost beside the point.

Almost. Our worldview that people, especially men, are inherently good, has changed.

You can #NotAllMen us—and by all means, feel free—because we already know there are good, even great, men who would never hurt us. If you're reading this, you're probably one of them. I'm not talking to you or including you in this conversation. This isn't about you.

The Rape

I haven't previously shared my own rape story; I'll do so here for the first time.

Trigger warning

I met a man for sex, something *I'm allowed to do* as an adult. I'd separated from my ex and wanted to explore, so I did. We'd met twice before, and it was good. Complete opposite of my ex—big guy, skillful. We discussed upfront what I was okay with and what I had no interest in. He was smart; he built trust.

I trusted my instincts. My bad.

When he became violent with me, engaging in painful sex acts I never consented to, I froze. I dissociated. Despite my desperate pleas to stop, he ignored me and continued till he finished.

As I lay limp as a ragdoll, he picked me up and put me in the shower, washing away all possible evidence, and then walked me to my car, ordering me not to tell a soul or he would send his brothers after my kids and me.

Terrified and shaking, I don't remember how I made it home—only what happened. I couldn't unsee it. I still can't. I kept replaying it all in my head. This is a common reaction to extreme trauma. Our brains are flooded with chemicals during any kind of intense, traumatic situation, in particular during a sexual assault. I went into survival mode.

I shut down. I didn't share with family or friends. I stopped dating, my body recoiling at the thought of any kind of touch. My skin crawled with every flashback. I cried constantly.

It took me months to share with anyone, and even then, only my therapist. I didn't use the word "rape" because I blamed myself.

"I put myself in that ... situation. It's my own fault," I told her, voice shaking. *"How can I call it ... rape?"*

"It's not your fault, honey," she soothed. *"You went there for consensual sex, agreed to in advance. He gained your trust. He didn't gain consent to hurt you."*

Self-blame. Humiliation. Embarrassment. **This** is why many of us don't disclose. I still feel like it's my own fault and yet, from a logical, even legal perspective, I *know* it's not.

I did not rape myself. I did not perpetrate criminal acts on myself. I am not a rapist. He is.

Should I have reported him? Tough one, and here's why I didn't
—terror. For me and my children. Judge me if you want—you can't
possibly reach the level of judgment I've already placed on myself.

Sharing this here with you is like a betrayal of my heart. I'm
waiting for the inevitable fallout.

It's no secret that many sexual abuse survivors wrestle with
mental health issues as a direct result of the trauma we experienced.
As a childhood sexual abuse survivor at age eleven, I experienced
panic attacks, anxiety, hypervigilance, and depression—not under-
standing or knowing these terrifying feelings had names (or even a
diagnosis of PTSD).

What many people have no understanding of is exactly how
trauma, especially sexual trauma, affects the brain of a survivor.
Which is why, when the more uneducated among us tell us to, "Just
get over it already," we'd *love* to. Alas, our brains, our very cells, don't
comply.

"Comprehensive systematic review and meta-analysis of 37
longitudinal observational comparative studies including 3,162,318
participants found an association between a history of sexual abuse
and a lifetime diagnosis of *anxiety, depression, eating disorders, PTSD, sleep
disorders, and suicide attempts.*[1]"

Multiple studies in epigenetics (DNA) show the brains of trauma
survivors actually change as a result of these experiences and can
even be passed down to future generations.

Triggers

You may be familiar with this word as a funny kind of game trolls
play on social media. For survivors, it's something else entirely. We
can be going about our day and then *boom*! We're hit with a flash-
back, scent, or news story that brings us right back into the trauma
we experienced.

This is our brain on trauma. Despite every effort we've made to
"just get over it and move on," we cannot control triggers that pop up
out of nowhere.

Officially defined, "a **trigger** in **psychology** is a stimulus such as a smell, sound, or sight that ***triggers*** feelings of trauma. People typically use this term when describing posttraumatic stress (PTSD)[2]."

For any survivor, this makes sense. For any non-survivor, I can tell you from experience, this makes no sense.

Example: My kids love horror movies. I do not. They recently played music from a horror movie after dinner, and I suddenly jumped up and yelled.

"Turn it off! Turn it off right now!"

"Okay. Geez. What's your problem?" my daughter asked, wide-eyed with incredulity (you see, I am *not* a yeller).

"I don't know. I don't know. I don't know! Just make it stop!" I answered, shaking uncontrollably. I left the room, bolted upstairs, focusing on my breathing till I calmed down.

Even I had no idea why that bothered me so. Talking it through with my guy helped. Hearing that scary music put me right back into that mind space of waiting to be victimized as a child. Waiting for the bad guy to get me—again. Of being that innocent child who had to hold that horrible secret—again.

It wasn't conscious on my part, yet that music became a trigger for me, bewildering my children.

Consciously, I didn't know. Subconsciously, I cannot un-know.

The #MeToo Movement

The #MeToo movement has opened the doors for many survivors to come forward after years, even decades, of not saying a word about what they experienced. Most childhood sexual abuse victims don't disclose until well into adulthood—if they disclose at all —with a median age of 48 and an average age of 52.

Hearing others' stories creates a compelling sense of courageous bravery we haven't seen before, a sort of receptiveness we hope will make a difference in how we're treated. As we've seen, sadly, this is not always the case, particularly, when famous men are involved (Jackson, Kavanaugh, Cosby, and Weinstein, just to name a few).

. . .

Sharing Our Stories

If you've read my previous books, *Broken Pieces* and *Broken Places*, or any of my blog or Medium posts, you know this about me: *I write what scares me*. I tell uncomfortable truths. I want other survivors of rape and sexual assault to know they're not alone.

I'll be the voice.

I am the voice.

Despite non-survivors telling us how terrible we are for coming forward years later or not reporting, or attempting to blame us for lying or gold-digging or fame, we know.

We were there.

We live it daily through PTSD, flashbacks, nightmares, holding our bodies rigid and primed for another assault. Through not trusting, not giving people a chance, never fully relaxing. Through anxiety, panic, depression, migraines, and a host of immune disorders we're much more susceptible to because of extreme trauma.

Healing is possible, with a trauma-trained therapist, support, community, and (for me) meds. Every survivor must find their own path. I find that researching and understanding what others experience is hugely helpful—to know we're not alone.

Sometimes I want to hug tightly to the innocence of non-survivors who make these victim-blaming statements and thank them for their insistent disbelief. How nice it must be to live in that bubble of smug sureness that the person they know (or think they know) would never, could never, abuse, assault, or rape someone.

Because survivors know, and we can never un-know.

*I used **she** statements because I'm a woman and I'm writing from *my perspective as a female survivor*; however, I recognize all genders are survivors and support all survivors.

---

1. Chen, Laura P, M Hassan Murad, Molly L Paras, Kristina M Colbenson, Amelia L Sattler, Erin N Goranson, Mohamed B Elamin, et al. "Sexual Abuse and Lifetime Diagnosis of Psychiatric Disorders: Systematic Review and Meta-Analysis." Mayo Clinic proceedings. Mayo Foundation for Medical Education and Research, July 2010. https://www.ncbi.nlm.nih.gov/pmc/articles/PMC2894717/.

2. Formatter, please place footnote with this citation:
    "The Psychology of Triggers and How They Affect Mental Health." Good-
    Therapy.org Therapy Blog. GoodTherapy, May 2, 2018. https://www.
    goodtherapy.org/blog/psychpedia/trigger.

The Day Is Worried

The day is worried about me.
Reaching out in fingered waves to hold me steady
but it's no use
I'll not be walking through her garden of green tendrils today,
I don't know the way.
Feet slipping on rust and golden leaves,
my hand slow dances for purchase
finding only air.

The day is worried about me.
Enveloping me in her cloudy blanket,
one I toss away
white wool too heavy today when
I can't find my breath.
Searching for the pull of his light
to bring me home.

The day is worried about me.
She can't find me in my usual places
hiding away
from myself today,

flashing green eyes hiding locked-door secrets
even I can't understand …
Maybe I'll find my key
as the day morphs into night.

The night is worried about me.
He can't hold me in his arms
I am transparent, slipping away in my quiet way,
weightless, floating
further from his grasp
until my Night-Man throws out his anchor
catching this desolate girl, pulling her close;
safe in his strong, capable arms.

Watching worries chase stars across the sky.

Running Away is Okay, As Long as We Come Back

"Because no matter where you run, you just end up running into yourself."
Truman Capote, Breakfast at Tiffany's[1]

Remember that '80s song by Flock of Seagulls about running so far away? If you lived through the '80s, you couldn't get away from it. I loved that song, even when I couldn't stand it anymore. It resonated with me on a deep level, one I wouldn't understand for many, many years. Decades, even.

Because I ran. Because I run. Because I still run.

Let me explain.

When I was eleven, a neighbor's dad sexually abused me and a few other neighbor girls. He was in the military. It happened more than once, so many more times than once, and I didn't understand what it was or why this thing, this monster, wanted me, what he wanted with me. Eventually, all our experiences with him came to light, and I testified against him in both civil and military trials. He got about *two years*, lost his pension, then moved back home.

My family didn't move away, so I lived with what happened for the next eight years until I left for college. I didn't receive therapy, and my family just kind of swept it under the rug. I lived with his kids' accusatory stares every day as I hurried to and from the same school, as if *I* were the one who had committed the crime. I lived with their rumors, gossip, and bullying as I rushed through my school activities, busy with busy-ness, terrified my friends would find out if I came to a standstill for even a moment.

So, I ran. I ran from the shame.

I never shared my story publicly until I wrote about it in my best-selling third book, *Broken Pieces*, in 2013, and my fourth book, *Broken Places*, in 2015. These are heavy books, filled with essays and poetry that discuss what it's like to live with the effects of being a survivor, as well as love and loss. Heavy books filled with light, and I hope, hope.

One of those effects is that I run—not the literal "put on your shoes and go for a run"—which I did for a long time until my knees gave out. No, this is a different kind of running. The kind that happens when I find myself in an emotionally overwhelming situation. I cut and run. I leave the room, and if I can't leave, I clam up. I'm Baby, put in the corner.

Until recently, I didn't know this is a common response for survivors of sexual abuse, and yet, it's not a bad thing. It seems like it would be, right? But it's not. You know why? Because it's a way for us to take back our power. *It's okay to run*, or in other words, to remove ourselves from a situation in which we are uncomfortable. We weren't able to do this when the abuse happened, so all these years of being scolded for being a coward or not standing up and "taking it" mean shit because I was actually strong! Just not in the usual way.

The trick here is that I would come back and resolve it (if I felt it was important enough), and that's what survivors have to decide for themselves. How important is the relationship?

Point is, it's okay to run, as long as we come back to form a resolution.

I won't lie; running from difficult situations has caused problems in my personal relationships. I'm now divorced after twenty-two years of marriage, and the man I'm with now gets very frustrated when I walk away from confrontation. He's a Scorpio—he loves to dig in and get things resolved *right then and there*. I'm the complete opposite (Capricorn, introvert), but it's a minefield once we add the past abuse. We're working through it, and his love and compassion for me helps immensely. So does this realization about running.

See, you have to understand something: I'm not a doormat or a victim. I speak my mind. I'm a strong woman—a feminist, and an advocate for women and children, particularly survivors of sexual abuse—but that doesn't mean I'm infallible.

For a long time, I, much like my family, minimized what happened. They believed me; how could they not? I testified in court —twice. There are plenty of court records around, as well as old neighbors I'm still in touch with today who came to court for support. I helped put the beast away. Still, the minimization was brutal. The family mantra became, "Rachel's abuse wasn't as bad as the others." I can't even get my mind around that to this day.

I became the good girl, the cheerleader, the overachiever who graduated college early, who got every award and promotion, who moved across the country alone to get that home office job. I was the one who ran, exhausted and panting for air, and who kept running because that's what I did. That's what I knew. That was my normal.

Until it all crashed down when I had my first baby—postpartum depression and terrifying anxiety. How can I ever let her out of my sight? This precious life that depends on me to keep her safe … what if I fail her? I finally started therapy and medication. Everything—all my freak outs and missteps and fears—started to make sense.

Our past doesn't just fall away, no matter how deeply we bury it.

I don't use my past as an excuse, but it does help me understand much more about my own behaviors and why I subconsciously react to situations the way I do. Becoming aware of the subconscious helps me deal with all of it in a more conscious way, if that makes sense. Being aware of why I react the way I do to situations is incredibly eye-opening and is part of the reason I write my books. Writing about the abuse so openly has been a wonderful way to connect with other survivors as well, to comprehend so much about what eluded me for so long.

Survivors, just like anyone, need to set boundaries. If putting the brakes on an emotionally difficult situation helps you, then do it.

Being aware of that is a big step. Run if you have to. And it's okay. Just be sure to come back to those people who mean something in your life because, if you don't, you'll have nothing, and maybe no one, to run back to.

---

1. Capote, Truman. Breakfast at Tiffany's and Three Stories. Saint Joseph, MO: Rolling Hills Consolidated Library, 2015.

I Am An Idiot

Here's what happens when you end a long-term relationship: The person you thought you loved becomes someone else entirely. Or is it because you become someone else?

I don't have the answer to that, but my guess is: probably.

You loved him. For decades. You put up with his foibles, weirdness, and obsessions because it's unique and makes him quirky. Kinda like your cat.

He gives what he thinks you need, you do the same, as years blindly bury attraction. Eventually, you decide the way he speaks to himself in third person/past tense about things that haven't even happened yet is, well, weird. Or that he takes stories you read to him from the paper as part of his own history as kinda, well, yeah—strange and off-putting.

And when you ask him for advice and he says, "You should do this," instead of hearing what you wanted advice about? Maybe he isn't listening at all.

You might finally realize being flat broke and in debt with mouths to feed, with the IRS knocking at your door isn't so fascinating (after all). You'll ask him how all this could have happened without your knowledge. He lights a fire under you by saying, "You knew all along."

You shake your head, and wonder ... did I?

Did I know but not see? Did I see but not know?

I am an idiot.

Write that across my heart. Scrawl it across the luggage I carry everywhere I go, heavy and broken, full of regrets.

I never believed in regrets before. A bold statement of the young. You make decisions and off you go. Can't change 'em. Shit happens, cookies crumble, milk spills.

If I could go back, would I? A stupid hypothetical, void of children who fill my desolate soul. Big round eyes, hearty laughs, and soft cheeks I die for. My babies, my loves, my life.

Yes, I've changed. I've become someone else. Someone who feels and gives and desires.

Someone who deserves.

Shoes

Burning with silence,
scars peeling with the layered skin of blistering years.
Words of pain dance in the moonlight,
fireflies spark with their grim mission
swollen with despair.

Why didn't you tell?
Why didn't you speak up?
Why wait? Why now?
Scorching shame roils inside humiliating waves of scorn and derision
as if we wanted to ever attend that party.

Not: *Why did he hurt her?*
Not: *Why did he abuse?*
But: *She must want money, attention or fame!*
Oh yes, that was my dream at age eleven
when a tall, huge, strange man forced me to do things
which had no name.

Catch this heavy ball—

carry this unbearable weight for just one day
then tell me all about my convenient motivations,
the timing of my "lies."
I'm unable to walk in your Shoes of Rationalization.
because they will never fit.

The Gray

I worked a sales job I hated for a good nine years. Every day, I'd wake up, spend hours getting ready, applying meticulous makeup, choosing just the right outfit, making sure my notes and records and routes were in order.

And then I'd go back to bed.

I'd lie there, fighting with myself. "Get up, you lazy bitch! What's wrong with you?" Berating myself for every imaginable slight. It was a well-paying job, one people yearn for, build up to after years of crap sales jobs, one that required not only a college degree but also a minimum of five to seven years of successful sales experience.

I not only had the supposed golden job, I excelled at it, won awards for "The Best" this and "The Top" that, where the European and New York heads chose me to work with when they visited my state. And, of course, I charmed them. My bosses were thrilled. I'd even managed a few sweet Ritz-Carlton dinners out of those visits.

Eventually, I roused myself out of my safe, cozy nest of blankets and sheets, wiped the tears and black streaks from my face (pro tip: use waterproof mascara), fixed my bedhead hair, and walked out the door.

But depression sneaks up on you.

I called on one of my physicians' office one bright, sunny day and dragged my dark, gloomy shell in to see one of them, a compassionate family practitioner who told me I didn't seem myself. Most of these doctors enjoy seeing sales reps as much as they enjoy dealing with insurance companies, but once in a while, you meet a jewel.

She took me inside a patient room and asked me what was up. I don't know if the fact she treated me like a human and not "another rep" did me in, or that I was simply just tired of the effort, but I became a sobbing mess (typical of many untreated depressives, by the way).

"Girl, you are depressed. I treat working moms every day. I'm not going to treat you because I'm not your doc and it wouldn't be ethical, but you need to get your ass into your own primary care for meds if needed (it's needed) and start therapy ASAP."

I'm depressed. *Duh.* Though my college degree was a BA in communication studies with a minor in journalism studies, I somehow ended up in sales for Big Pharma. There was a lot of biology, pharmacology, and the like to learn, and though my company sold SSRIs, I personally did not sell them (though all reps did learn about them in case a physician asked).

How could I not have seen it? The symptoms I experienced were classic:
- Not wanting to be around other people
- Neglecting everyday tasks or struggling to do them
- Loss of interest in activities I once enjoyed or struggling to do them
- Intense sadness/crying that just won't fade
- Unresolved anger

Still, I kept going as if nothing were wrong ... until it was *so* wrong.

I spoke with my husband who owned his own business at the time and discussed different job options for me. I wanted to do something different where I could spend more time with our small daughter, utilize my writing and marketing skills (which I loved), and still bring in money.

His response? *"Well, you'll have to just suck it up. You're the one with the time and regular benefits. You have the security. You may hate it but, but you know, too bad."*

He's no longer my husband.

Eventually, after I began to spend more days in bed than working, even *he* couldn't deny I needed help. Despite his reservations (he believed SSRIs would make me a zombie), he encouraged me to go to a shrink. Thankfully, I ended up with a good one who immediately started me on a regimen of therapy and meds.

The gray lifted within a week and continued to lift as the weeks went on. Therapy helped immensely as well.

I still hated my job—I was clearly a creative square in a round corporate hole—but I could at least get out of bed, go to work, and joke around with my doctors. Maybe it wasn't so important to be the best all the time. I didn't cry at the thought of being away from my daughter, though I still didn't enjoy it. (Who does?)

I began to make an exit strategy from this hell of a job.

In therapy, Dr. G asked me some basic questions, and I answered honestly; he didn't want me to cover up anything. One of the most glaring examples for me that something was wrong would happen whenever we used our season passes to take our daughter to Disneyland. I shrank from the noise and ended up crying on a bench while she and my husband laughed and enjoyed themselves.

Why was I crying at The Happiest Place on Earth? Who does that?

Eventually, I told my therapist my entire story. Stopping and starting, voice shaking with trepidation, I almost robotically (and clearly dissociating) explained what had happened to me as a young girl. I'd seen him for months before I broached this thorny topic, yet I floated across the room as I released this information from my bones. No longer terrified, my soul lifted, freed from hiding this heavy part of myself from this skilled, compassionate man who was doing his best to help me.

He said the diagnosis was obvious: I'd lived with anxiety, depression, and PTSD until my mid-thirties. I had dealt with all of these mental disorders until it came crashing down.

I didn't know. I had no idea. Nobody around me knew either.

It's kind of astounding that I worked in the healthcare industry and had no knowledge of how what I'd experienced as a child could affect me. As a society, our focus is so much on the physical ailments people live with daily that even when someone is diagnosed with a mental disorder, we still look for physical manifestations.

Why did I hate this job so much? Good job, great benefits. Why did I feel I so angry about it? Misplaced anger. We had problems in the marriage—I felt stuck, and my partner clearly didn't support my needs. To be fair, he hadn't disclosed to me he had a failing business which eventually crumbled completely, leaving us in financial ruin.

I quit that job and never looked back. I had another child, moved away, started my writing career, founded BadRedhead Media (my social media/marketing business) and divorced the husband.

For perspective, my daughter will be twenty-two in July. So, what lessons have I learned in the time since she was a baby, and I was crying at Disneyland?

First, the combination of the right medicine and talk therapy helped me immensely, and it's still something I actively utilize today. Journaling has also been incredibly helpful for me, both personally and therapeutically. (You know, writers write.)

Second, there's absolutely no shame in asking for help, realizing you need it, and most importantly, if the people around you don't support your mental health, make those hard decisions whether to keep them in your life. I also learned large crowds and unsupportive partners are not good for my mental health, so I avoid both.

Only you can decide what's best for your mental health, but that's the key right there: Pay attention and decide because you are worth it.

How My Divorce Made Me A Better Person

Many times, after people divorce, you hear stories about how it becomes a chilling war between the two people, or perhaps you've witnessed it yourself as a child of divorce, or you've seen movies or read books about it. As the daughter of parents who've been together over sixty years, I have gratefully never experienced that type of animosity as their child.

But my kids have.

When my ex and I were smug marrieds, we made a pact after seeing our friends go through The Divorce Uglies. *If* we ever split, we'd always put the kids first, we promised one another in our quiet little beach garden after too many dry chardonnays and cigarettes, our only witnesses the bright birds of paradise with their chirpy, knowing eyes.

No tug-of-war, no alimony, share everything 50/50, we promised one another. We kissed on it.

Ah, the naïveté.

I'm not here to trash my ex. We're four years out now, and I've learned some hard lessons. Brutal truths about both him and I that used to burn my throat as I swallowed the unspoken.

Here are my tips for getting through this fire.

. . .

Accept there is no winning in divorce.

Regardless of whether one of you is awarded custody, child support, or alimony, the reality is that the emotional and psychological toll of all those years of discord combined with the entire shake-up of your new life without your partner (freeing as it may be) wreaks unexpected havoc on you and your children (if you have them).

Change is difficult, even when you welcome it. I waited and waited, hoping talking and therapy would help. Tsk, I know. It didn't.

I pictured how it would feel telling my ex to leave and filing the papers, as if I'd fly across the water, wings stretching so far, I'd reach both water and sky.

We'd been together over two decades, had two children together. Telling him to leave took months of arduous planning. Sitting down with him, hands shaking and heart pounding with fear, I formed words in an almost comical slow-motion.

It wasn't comical. It didn't feel like flying. It felt like a crushing death.

And that makes sense, right? We grieve for endings, for what could have been that didn't end the way we expected. Once I accepted that freeing myself from him didn't have to feel like flying but more like grounding, I embraced the slower pace of moving forward.

You will feel angry

When two people split, whatever codependent, screwed-up routines that got you through the days and long nights are now Gonesville. Your everyday normal is anything but. As tiny humans, we crave routine. It's how we thrive. As adults, we are slightly more adaptable, but not much.

A tired, hungry child will act out. Adults aren't much different.

Throw in exhaustion and worry about finances and now lawyer's fees, children, and other emotional bullshit … we quickly rise to anger. Everything that's going wrong is the other person's *fault*. If you're a parent, kids see this, and it becomes even more difficult to regulate our emotions.

This is the tricky part. It's so easy to place blame. And where does that get us? (See Point #1 above: There is no winning.) The ugly truth is, the fault lies in all of us. None of us is perfect (come on, who is?).

What do we do with all this rage? Where does it come from—figuring out the details of the separation/divorce? How does blaming our partner help in any way? You know the answer. It doesn't.

What to do?

- **Therapy helps incredibly.** Now is not the time to suck it up. Speak to a neutral party. Your friends, family, and potential dates are *not* interested. Believe me.
- **A good lawyer** (or mediator).
- **Exercise.** Burn it off with some kind of cardio. Kickboxing or running are especially helpful. Yoga, if you're more like me—meditative with bad knees.
- **Writing.** My saving grace. Whether it's public or not, it doesn't matter. Journal any way that works for you, blog it out, write poetry or fiction, whatever. If you decide you want to write a book about it all at some point, fine. Don't worry about that now. Don't fear it. Just write.

Own your shit and learn from it.

Even if your ex is an abusive mofo or the high school sweetheart you will always love, it's helpful to look at *where you are now* and learn from the experience. The past and your history will always be there.

Regardless of what your spiritual beliefs are (I'm not particularly religious myself, having traded Bat Mitzvah and Hebrew classes for cheerleading and gymnastics), there is some truth to finding our way through our various life experiences (good and bad) and understanding why things happen.

In truth, we may never know the "why's;" however, we can learn so much about ourselves and how we reacted to these experiences. Therapy is crucial here.

Perhaps you both contributed to the dissolution of your marriage in some way. *To be clear,* I'm not discussing domestic abuse situations or victim-blaming. I dealt with my own abusive situation

There it is. It's easy to blame my ex for whatever he did, or whatever I couldn't accept about him, or whatever he does now that drives me crazy.

We divorced for a reason.

Past, present, and future all merge into this heavy weight I no longer want to carry. And I don't have to, so I don't. My choice.

It takes distance, courage, and acceptance to realize how my codependent contributions and anger toward him made things worse. I don't mean that I accept that I *deserved* any of his unacceptable behaviors toward me. In fairness, he didn't deserve whatever I said or did to him. We made situations difficult and hurt each other.

I know *now* that not engaging is a better choice. I own that.

You will be stronger.

Divorce, for some, is like a death. We're allowed to mourn a life we had that ends. It explodes our routine world, which throws our ordered life out of balance. Change is scary, man. So is chaos.

A work colleague told me she didn't think she'd ever recover from her divorce because her husband rejected her in the most brutal way. This beautiful (like, stunning), brilliant single mother of two says her self-esteem is shot. Now she's involved with a struggling artist/addict. We both know she deserves better.

She'll get there. Being beautiful and smart doesn't mean she doesn't suffer. Not the point. It means we all walk through this fire in our own ways, yet there's no getting around it.

Eventually, we find out who we are because we are on our own in such a vast myriad of ways.

I learned exactly how strong I am as a woman, mother, and human because of this experience. I've earned my mettle. As I said in the beginning, there is no winning in divorce. Sure, I've won my freedom; though, in my bones, I already had that.

What I learned was how to accept all that comes with it.

Perfect Victim

I sometimes sit here in agony with flashbacks and nightmares, jump-scared at every loud noise. So many people, though, sit on their thrones of snide judgment, daring to tell survivors that what caused all this is untrue because … why?

"You so-called 'survivors' lie all the time."

"False reports are far more common than people realize."

"Women abuse far more than men do."

What's in it for them to deny the fact I—along with millions of others—are survivors (all genders) of sexual crimes?

Please, explain this to me. I'm at a loss.

I want to share the story of Hannah Gavios[1], a female runner shoved off a running trail in Thailand by a rapist. She tumbled hundreds of feet to the bottom where she lay in agony with a broken spine, praying not to die. The man who pushed her then raped her repeatedly and left her for dead. She survived with partial paralysis, identified him, and eventually used crutches to "run" the New York Marathon in 2018.

Truly a hero's story! An inspiration.

Every news outlet that reported this story focused on the physical difficulties she had to overcome to complete the marathon, and it was major. She dedicated her life to completing this goal. I'm in awe of her.

What I found interesting was, not one story discussed the emotional and psychological effects of surviving a brutal rape; of almost dying; of being left for dead in a foreign country after a brutal sexual assault with a potentially life-ending injury. What kind of therapy did she undergo? Does she suffer from PTSD? (Maybe she chose not to discuss any of this; that's a legit choice.)

I also found it interesting that many of the people who reject sexual assault claims of survivors because there's "no proof," embraced this young woman's story because her devastating physical injuries provided the proof they needed. I read their comments of amazement and support. She deserves that support. Please understand I'm in no way attempting to take away anything from her.

Here's what sickens me: Her body is now hopelessly mangled, so boom—proof!—the naysayers believe she was sexually assaulted.

Her word alone is not enough.

If one were to take away the horrific, unimaginable horror this young woman lived through, would they still believe her? Doubtful. Child molesters, rapists, and sexual assaulters abuse millions of victims and people don't believe us because many survivors don't appear to be forever physically damaged.

But we are. More on that in a moment.

How *sick* is this? How *sad* is this? I feel revulsion just writing this.

Prickling stabs of guilt weighed on me for even thinking these thoughts, so I reached out to my brilliant survivor friend, Ryan, because I would never want to take away from the joy of her achievement. Hannah Gavios is a role model for many survivors of rape and sexual assault. She was able to turn something horrible into something positive. Amazing.

Ryan reminded me it's okay to feel revolted by how Gavios has physical damage, yet people still don't believe her. He talked to me about our conflicting emotions because some survivors will never get to the place she is. (She was already an avid, competitive runner before the assault.) Returning to running in whatever form she is able is probably therapeutic for her (an assumption, clearly). All survivors must find healing in our own way.

According to the American Psychiatric Association, many survivors suffer physical difficulties after sexual assault, often due to PTSD.

> *"We can experience increased blood pressure and heart rate, fatigue, muscle tension, nausea, joint pain, headaches, back pain or other types of pain. The person in pain may not realize the connection between their pain and a traumatic event. An estimated one in 11 people will be diagnosed PTSD in their lifetime. Women are twice as likely as men to have PTSD.*
>
> *For people with chronic pain, the pain may actually serve as a reminder of the traumatic event, which in turn may intensify PTSD symptoms. Some people who develop PTSD and chronic pain also experience depression and alcohol and prescription medication misuse. Chronic PTSD has been shown to increase the risk of having a variety of health issues and decreased life expectancy.*[2]*"*

Therapists say anger is a secondary emotion. I am angry. Angry at the people who victim-blame. So, what is my secondary emotion? What do most survivors feel first? Typically, hurt or fear. Hurt at not being believed. Fear at the loss of control. Valid emotions, all of them.

There's often an endless hill to climb as a survivor—not only our own mental, emotional, and physical battles but also those we take on to help our fellow survivors against those who victim-blame. I find joy in our triumphs, whether it's obvious, like Ms. Gavios, or another survivor who got out of bed and made it to the shower.

Compassion is the answer. How we get there is the question.

---

1. Dam, TuAnh. "Sexual Assault Survivor Completes NYC Marathon in Crutches." Yahoo! Finance. Yahoo!, November 6, 2018. https://finance.yahoo.com/news/sexual-assault-survivor-completes-nyc-marathon-crutches-064826741.html.
2. Parekh, Ranna. "What Is Posttraumatic Stress Disorder?" What Is PTSD? American Psychiatric Association, January 2017. https://www.psychiatry.org/patients-families/ptsd/what-is-ptsd.

Earth

We've Lived in Shame Long Enough

I kiss my boy before he turns to his friends, leaving me with his innocence and sweet, soft cheeks. He runs off for a day of fun and learning ... imagination his natural ally. My boy, a dreamer, loves to be my protector when it suits him until nighttime fears swallow him up in the dark. Then, he snuggles tightly into me, afraid of the unknown.

But I know.

I pass an old brown El Camino parked in a random driveway every morning when I drive my boy to school and back. My heart races and my foot accelerates. I can't move past that foreign—yet familiar—car fast enough.

The car reminds me of a monster that and kept his El Camino parked in the driveway next door. I was barely older than my boy when the monster trapped me in his nest of scooter rides and lollipops. He had a daughter my age and often offered an invitation to come over and play in a cold swimming pool on a brutally hot day. Opportunities.

Monsters know what children crave, and sadly, the reverse often becomes true.

I didn't share what happened to me until I had to—when the sheriffs knocked at our door. I didn't say anything then, either, because of the shame. Shame is a powerful emotion, stronger than fear. I often wonder what it takes to be a police officer and to have to coax a story out of child mired in shame so thick they reek of it. That child-like scent of innocence and purity you can smell in their sweet hair, gone.

What happened to you wasn't as bad as what happened to the other, smaller girls.

There were trials. I testified twice—yes, twice—in civil and military lawsuits because he was a military officer, and he carried a gun. I was old enough to testify, to verbalize what he had done. He went to jail for two years and lost his pension.

My family continued to live next door to his family for many more years. I went to school with his children, even after he returned. A glass wall of silence shattered with glares of hate, as if I had done the crime. I was gone as soon as I could move out for college.

In my strenuous efforts to deal with it all, I dissociated by immersing myself in athletics and school and boys and weed and … whatever could keep me busy. I was numb. Flashbacks, nightmares, PTSD, panic—all of this encompassed my growing up since I didn't have names for these things.

Deal with it; it wasn't that bad. It could have been worse.

Depression and anxiety hit with a vengeance once I gave birth to my first child in my mid-thirties. What if the same thing happened to my baby daughter? How could I keep her safe? I started to spin and, eventually, became inconsolable, incapable of functioning outside of that mindset. I sought help. Thirty years after my experience with the monster, I finally, *finally* realized I needed help. That child, my sweet, loving, artistic daughter, is in her early-twenties, and my boy is in high school. Wow.

I am overprotective and I'm okay with that. My children know I was sexually abused when I was eleven. They don't know the extent because they don't need to. They know I have written books about my experience and that I started #SexAbuseChat_on Twitter. They also know I've created @SpeakOurStories with Dr. Shruti Kapoor with the goal of bringing stories of trauma and recovery to life. It doesn't mean all that much to them, and that's okay too. "Mom is a writer and stuff," my boy tells his friends.

It's okay they don't really understand the gravity of everything

that happened to me because I want them to maintain their inno-
cence as long as they can. For a long time, they still clung to their
belief in Santa Claus, though my daughter called him Sketchy Claus.
It's good to laugh about such things.

There's not always justice in this world. Monsters still exist, chil-
dren are still abused. Awareness is greater now than when I was a
kid, and if I have had some small part in that, whether it's through
my books, or being an outspoken advocate for children and survivors,
then I'm honored.

All I know is, ***every survivor has a right to tell our
story*** because we did nothing wrong.

We've lived in shame long enough.

Green Eyes

I also said no at first.

When the police asked if our neighbor touched me inappropriately, I said no, as my skin crawled with the feeling of his fingers making their invading way into my soul.

I said no.

Sweat beaded down my neck, tiny baby hairs sticky with guilt. I looked up at my mother, my large, green eyes spilling with secrets too big to hold. Eyes that had seen a man's cock, felt it press against my back while riding his scooter with the wind in my hair, desiring that little bit of freedom, never realizing the payment due.

Squirming away from his inevitable grasp, desolation pressed against my chest. I could not breathe.

I stood mute, mesmerized, watching the policeman's mouth moving around the word "inappropriately." Memories filter through my eyes in waves, a silent call for help, even as my mouth formed the word "no."

Eyes are such betrayers of truth.

Shame thought she was my friend, keeping me safe in her silence, cocooned in the quiet knowledge of shared secrets. She didn't mean to make me feel bad or dirty or used. She only wanted to protect me from humiliation, never realizing how keeping me alone created even more terror.

Shame is still sorry to this day.

I say no as Shame shines from my eyes, a beaconing glimpse into the unholy madness I hold inside, opening a sliver of release in me.

Holding my hand, Shame gently walks me to that monolithic door of truth ...

Where I cry, yes.

Uncomfortable Truths

A man once asked me if writing books about my abuse isn't an exercise in self-indulgence. In his opinion, he felt sharing my experiences of childhood sexual abuse and its aftereffects—or as he put it, talking about myself in memoir form—is "whining." Others have referred to it as "trauma porn."

I wasn't offended. This is a common perception (um, misperception) from many non-survivors, both male and female. It's also representative of a general societal attitude that—from the perspective of the survivor—any kind of sex crimes should remain private. Topics of sex make people uncomfortable, regardless of the amount of advertising and the number of popcorn media based on the topic, regardless of the fact that sexual assault isn't sexual.

As we all know, sex sells, right? Not so fast. [12]

"*Researchers analyzed the results of 53 different experiments (a meta-analysis) involving nearly 8,500 people, done over 44 years. All of these experiments examined some facet of the question of whether sexual or violent media content could help sell advertised products.*

When all the results are considered together, the overall conclusion, with some caveats, is that programs featuring violence and sex aren't the ideal context for effective advertising."

Am I therefore, in some way, capitalizing on sex by using it to sell books?

No, but I do see how someone could say that. Let's deconstruct.

When I published my first book, *Broken Pieces*, I had some of those same concerns: Is talking about what I experienced going to make people think I'm somehow a victim? Am I vain? Will they see my book(s) as some kind of vanity project?

Valid fears (for any writer). Those fears vanished quickly when survivors from all over the world reached out to me with their own survivor stories (via social media, email, and reviews). The reaction to that book was nothing short of overwhelming.

I also learned I cannot control how people react to my story or books. If they don't approve or like what I write about, that's not my issue. As I coach writers in the creative nonfiction workshops I teach, once our books are out there, we're no longer invited to the party.

From an educational standpoint, many non-survivors don't understand how the brain of a survivor is affected in the long-term.[3] And they don't care to know, don't believe it, or, and this is key, don't know what they don't know. When corrected, non-survivors who believe survivors lie about being raped or sexually assaulted (I mean, why), often immediately become defensive and attempt to prove their argument.

I don't engage with those folks. It's just not worth my time. I used to. It's important to me that survivors understand the effects of abuse and get the support we deserve. It's not important to listen to uneducated, ignorant armchair quarterbacks pontificate on a topic, particularly related to mental and emotional health. When I read this quote by Brené Brown, everything became crystalized: *We need to be selective about the feedback we let into our lives. For me, if you're not in the arena also getting your ass kicked, I'm not interested in your feedback.*

Is there any other crime where victims must prove our innocence? And why is that a standard of proof? Especially when it comes to babies and children. It's fucking sickening.

I had absolutely no idea what my abuser's intentions were as an eleven-year-old child. I didn't know about sex. Nothing. Nada. My parents did nothing more than hug or smooch in front of my sister and me. We didn't have the internet of things. We had no books or magazines to look at. (My father was a nerd—his idea of fun mags were *Stereo Review* and something about bowling.)

Accusing children of inviting predators to abuse us, which is what happens in courtrooms by defense attorneys who are doing their jobs, is beyond the pale. In my own experience testifying, facing my abuser in a courtroom (this was the 70s) made my bones quiver. Saying what he did to me made me want to hide behind the judge's robes. If a child cannot prove their innocence, the abuser walks free.

How can we create a solution? I don't have the answer, except to believe survivors. Innocent children don't lie about something they've never been exposed to. I literally did not have the verbiage to explain what my abuser did to me. That's clue number one. Nobody 'coached' me.

Protect your children. If you have concerns about someone who's around your child, trust your gut. Remove them from the situation. Don't worry about the semantics or social graces of it all. Better to lose a friend or relationships with a family member than your child be raped or assaulted and deal with a lifetime of mental health challenges! Learn more tips here.[4]

---

1. John G. Wirtz, Johnny V. Sparks & Thais M. Zimbres (2018) The effect of exposure to sexual appeals in advertisements on memory, attitude, and purchase intention: a meta-analytic review, International Journal of Advertising, 37:2, 168-198, DOI: 10.1080/02650487.2017.1334996
2. Staff. "Research Suggests Sexual Appeals in Ads Don't Sell Brands, Products." Phys.org. Science X, June 22, 2017. https://phys.org/news/2017-06-sexual-appeals-ads-dont-brands.html
3. Hopper, J. (n.d.). *Jim Hopper, Ph.D.* Jim Hopper PHD. http://www.jimhopper.com/
4. U.S. National Library of Medicine. (n.d.). *Sexual abuse in children - what to know: MedlinePlus Medical Encyclopedia.* MedlinePlus. https://medlineplus.gov/ency/patientinstructions/000771.htm.

The Ocean of Me

nobody gets to save me but me
nobody gets to save me but me
my mantra.

I learned that hard lesson at age eleven when I couldn't make
him stop
hands everywhere, lips and tongue invading my tiny, terrified body
I would have given anything just to make it stop

helplessness didn't help
so, I told. I testified.

eighteen months later, he came back.

for forty-three years, he's come back
to invade my mind
flashbacks
every day
flashbacks
nobody gets to save me but me
nobody gets to save me but me

who ever said life would be fair?
survivors survive. we save ourselves
I made it through the stinging, clawing, burning fire and now …
now I swim in the deep, blue ocean of me.

helplessness didn't help
so, I told. I testified.

eighteen months later, he came back.
for forty-six years, he's come back

maybe nobody gets to save me but me
maybe nobody gets to save me but me

I learned to ask for help
in this vast, blue ocean

I am not alone anymore
I am not alone anymore.

Lessons Learned

I recently learned a big lesson: Your body will literally purge the negative energy from your soul when you make a stand against someone.

Our bodies carry memories—wounds we may never fully recognize—yet they are there, waiting patiently to tap us on the shoulder.

We make the choice to accept or reject. I gather up the tattered ribbons and toss them in haste because I want to be free.

I needed to be out from under a weight so bulging and burdensome, I panicked with the thought of how to maneuver with it. So, I threw it off me fast, as if my hands were singed from a burning pan —pain hitting me, racing for the cold, clear water of relief.

Breath. Air. Calm.

When you let someone go, you not only release them, you release yourself.

I released me.

Truth

One of the main reasons I share my story about surviving childhood sexual abuse is so others won't feel alone. But there's another reason. I didn't understand the short-term and long-term effects this kind of trauma would have on me while I was growing up (honestly, nobody did).

It was why I checked my windows every night. Why I was convinced the next-door neighbor's dad (my abuser) would break in and kill my family or me with his gun. Why I had panic attacks. Why I developed migraines soon afterward, something I still have to this day. Why I became acutely self-conscious and extremely perfectionistic.

Why I still have many of these experiences, decades later.

The psychiatric and medical communities have only recently begun to understand how developing brains are affected—and this is forty-six years after my experience occurred.

I realize that asking the general public to have any concept of what trauma does to children (and even adults) is asking a lot, yet we are constantly bombarded by people who demand sexual abuse survivors "get over it," which is unbelievably callous as well as ignorant, yet not surprising.

An example from Twitter: "Getting picked last for dodge ball can be just as traumatic as rape, but you don't see me whining about it on social media."

Another example I received on Twitter: "Oh ffs. P*ss off with the trauma."

As I mention in *Broken Places*: just because survivors are open and share our experiences doesn't mean we are "whining." The issue here is most people have zero concept of trauma's biological, chemical, and physiological effects on survivors' brains and bodies—and now I understand why this is.

Unless you are a survivor, why would you care to find out?

Non-survivors make assumptions about what it's like to be us, when they know nothing whatsoever about it. Invalidating and minimizing another's criminal trauma, our lived experience, the narrative we never sought to own but now have branded on us for life, somehow makes them what? Feel better about themselves in some way?

Rape and childhood sexual abuse are not only criminal but are also considered crimes against humanity. Comparing sexual assault to being picked last for dodgeball is a false construct.

There's a certain strength of character to survivors that non-survivors will never experience, and good for them. I hope they never do. We are still here, and we are still fighting every day in ways they cannot fathom. Making negative comments about us is so … cute. I want to sit them down with my best resting bitch face and ask politely, "Do you know, can you even fathom, what we have been through?"

Comments which aim to denigrate us do nothing more than show a complete lack of character, as well as reinforce our magical powers.

Ahh. Muggles.

As with any situation, if it doesn't affect you personally, you likely have zero interest in it. Therein lies the issue. *Why are people who are not survivors commenting on what survivors should do? How we should feel? How we should react?*

Why do non-survivors care about how survivors live our lives? What's it to them?

I've been on a mission to learn and share as much information as possible about what trauma (any kind of trauma) does to survivor brains since I started writing my first *Broken* book back in 2010. I wanted to understand why I have daily flashbacks, anxiety, nightmares, depression, migraines, an acute startle response, and more. Would a non-survivor understand any of this?

You can't look at me and know, for the last *four decades*, I've had daily flashbacks of being sexually abused. Or that I haven't ever been able to have a man hold me while I go to sleep in any relationship, until my recent guy. Or that I wake up screaming in fear, or if my children slam a door, I jump three feet and inexplicably cry for an hour.

Or that I want to tell people "Live through this, motherfucker" when they compare the trauma of breaking a pencil lead to being raped.

I don't say any of that, though, because I don't want to bring people down. Because I don't want people's pity or for them to view me as fragile. Because there's more to me than "survivor." Because they don't *deserve* my resting bitch face.

Because they are not worthy.

More than anything, I want any survivor who is reading this to know they did nothing wrong. *We didn't sexually abuse ourselves.* I understand so much more now about living with the effects of trauma—with the fear, shame, and guilt, as well as the mental and physiological effects mentioned above—and now take an active part in my recovery, something I never understood was even possible before.

You are worthy. We are worthy. Of respect, love, and understanding. Of help. Ignore those random, ignorant trolls unless you can use them to help spread your message, as I have. Then by all means, have at it.

When Will People Stop Blaming Survivors of Sexual Trauma for Surviving?

** *Trigger Warning* **

The following contains graphic details of sexual abuse. It is not for attention or shock value. This is my story, and it needs to be told. I'm sorry you have to read what's next. It was hard to write, and I hope you will stay with me for the rest.

Do you know what it's like to be ordered to lick a man's penis "like an ice cream cone" when you're eleven years old? I can't imagine most of the population can comprehend that.

I can.

Because a man forced me to. More than once.

I didn't tell when the police eventually questioned me, after enduring more than a year of various forms of abuse. I was terrified this giant of a man who lived next door—a military man with a gun —would kill my baby sister, so I kept quiet. But my eyes dripped tears of tales untold, an admission of guilt owned by the intentions of men.

Eventually, I did tell and lived through two trials—taunting, haunting, harrowing trials that narrowed the world between he and I once again.

"How will I ever escape the confines of this man's world?" I wanted to scream, in words I didn't know how to utter as I testified twice before God and man and him, specifying in impolite, forensic detail the ways he abolished my soul.

Telling isn't justice, and justice isn't handed down when victim blaming is first on everyone's mind. Why are survivors forced to own our abusers' intentions? He got eighteen months and then moved back home—right next door and merely feet away from my window—for another eight years. Years of long, slow days full of his kids' accusatory stares and his wife's accusatory lips.

How will I ever escape the confines of this man's world?

People tell survivors we are somehow complicit if we don't tell. We are told he will hurt someone else if we keep quiet and it's somehow our fault he is a criminal who will continue to commit crimes.

We, as young, slight, innocent girls, are to blame for the behavior of men.

It's all very easy for non-survivors to make these statements. Do this, do that, and done. One, two, three. They cannot comprehend why we wouldn't want to tell.

Have you been online lately? The myriad of reasons survivors don't report is justifiable and lengthy: shame, fear of job loss, not being believed, minimizing our own experiences, bullying, ranking the abuse … it goes on. The worst part, however, is the verbal abuse people pile on, full of judgment about situations of which they know nothing.

The immensity of survival isn't so facile, though, is it? Even forty-three years later, the ulcerating pain in my stomach reminds me of the terror. The powerlessness as I slide into a dissociated state of nothingness, the only area of my being he cannot invade. I've learned from an early age to redirect to happier thoughts when I experience the daily flashbacks, so I don't break down into numbing blankness or worse, go back to his world. Again.

Some tell us it's on us, the "victim" (in the legal sense of the word) to not put ourselves in high-risk situations. We should "know better," particularly women, who may have worn a skirt one inch too high or a top one inch too low (because clothing creates the situation for rapists to rape, apparently), or who may have taken a business meeting that put us in a high-risk situation.

It amazes me the questions people ask me and other survivors of sexual trauma (particularly rape survivors), as if we had the intention of becoming the victims of sexual predators.

What were you wearing?
Why didn't you stop it or fight back?
Why didn't you tell anyone when it happened?
Where's the proof?

The issue here is, again, people relentlessly placing blame for a criminal's behavior on his victim, thus removing the responsibility for the crime from the criminal. In fact, the language here completely removes the criminal from the sentence. The onus is on the victim to not get raped, as opposed to the rapist to not rape.

Rachel was molested.
versus
The neighbor molested Rachel.

See the difference between those two sentences?

Let's flip that language, that paradigm, that fucked-up thought process. Let's ask these predators the right questions.

Why did you do it?
Why didn't you know it was wrong?
Why didn't you tell anyone you raped her?
Why didn't you stop?

Here's the reality of reporting our abuse: Statistically, most sexual crimes go unreported.[1] Those that do are rarely prosecuted. Defense lawyers go out of their way to discredit witnesses for lying, wanting attention, or being unreliable (particularly if they had been drinking). Yes, even eleven-year-old girls. What's so terribly sad is the end result. Victims don't come forward and report.

However, I'm not here to debate with those who claim victims are lying or that statistics are inflated, because people are not stats. I'm here to focus on survivors, and we will *not* be blamed.

The ignorance of those who blame survivors of sexual trauma for being survivors of sexual trauma lies in the fact they do not understand the crime itself is not about sexual gratification but about power. And sexual abuse, assault, rape, and harassment certainly aren't political acts. They are acts of control and they all cause harm. Hold abusers accountable not because of their politics but because of their crimes.

In my situation, at the age of eleven, I, along with a bunch of other neighborhood kids, took turns getting scooter rides with the Pied Piper. This guy had grooming down to a science. He gave us candy—it was fun and not something our parents did with us. He paid attention to us. He asked us questions. We mattered. Most non-survivors won't understand or take into consideration something like grooming, yet it's always part of an abuser's arsenal, particularly with young children. They make us feel special, wanted, and cherished.

Said the spider to the fly.

Sexual abuse of any kind is a conscious decision made by an abuser. Child molestation, sexual assault, and rape are crimes, make no mistake about it, and what happens to survivors is criminal. Regardless of what happens to our abuser, our sentence lasts for life. The effects of sexual trauma are long-term: PTSD, anxiety, depression, migraines, even immune disorders.

So why didn't I speak out initially, unprompted by police?

Terror, for one. I truly believed he would kill my baby sister, or worse, my entire family. He had a gun, and he told me he would use it.

Grooming, for another. He convinced me nobody would believe me, and why would I have reason to doubt an authority figure? He used my naïveté against me, as most abusers do. He also told me *I* would go to jail, and I believed him.

And finally, my introverted nature. Never a loud, gregarious child, I withdrew further into myself and my safe, imaginary, quiet world of stories, where little girls destroyed monsters, not the other way around.

In this impossible situation, this sick abuser stole my innocence, my being, my soul.

Eventually, I found all the scattered pieces and pulled myself back together. I was broken and chipped yet still capable of breaking through the enormous barriers of fear and shame to tell my story, and now I help others feel less alone.

We all heal in our own way. We all deserve to recover in our own way. Survivors don't need family, friends, and total strangers to blame us for crimes *we did not commit*. We don't sexually abuse ourselves. We don't want pity; we want support, compassion, help, and love.

For one tiny second, put yourself in my small shoes at the very beginning of this piece. Close your eyes and feel what I felt. Now, open your eyes.

Poof.

Gone.

It's nice to make that go away, isn't it?

Survivors can't do that. In the best of circumstances, we work through it, creating a good life just like anyone else. We can and do thrive.

Believe us. That's all we ask.

---

1. "The Criminal Justice System: Statistics." RAINN. Accessed April 19, 2020. https://www.rainn.org/statistics/criminal-justice-system.

Water

The Burn

When I finally decided it was time to tell my ex-husband I wanted him to move out, I wanted a divorce, the truth is, I wasn't ready to walk through the fire. Skipping around the burning coals for years, dancing past the cinders, dropping hints through smoke so thick it choked my ability to not only be honest with him but with myself.

Burying myself inside ramshackle, thorny pillars of daily survival —walking through each day without resentment, eating away at my growing scorn toward him became a sort of merciless victory. I knew it didn't feel right, not knowing why.

Drifting further into myself, the cloud of silence growing, the fire building.

When silence didn't work, we had conversations about what needed to change, what we both needed to work on. I loved him. It wasn't that. It's still not that. He's decent enough, a good father. I've known him almost half my life. My God, how is that possible?

Yet my feet continued to burn.

I blurted it out one day, "You need to leave!" in a rush before I lost my nerve, my soles on fire. I couldn't breathe with his booming voice anymore, his anxiety vibrating, snapping at the very air of his slamming-door, slamming-drawer, clutter-filled presence. I needed peace. I wanted counter space. To breathe in my own clear air.

My soul burned.

So, he left. Not without some protest, a mountain of bills, and the upheaval of our now suitcase-carrying, back and forth children who think I'm being selfish. That's okay. I see their point. They are too young to understand that breathing isn't selfish.

It's more important that we do this thing together, focusing on co-parenting them, and we are. We are stilted friends. He still calls me "Hon" after twenty-two years together, which is only slightly strange, just as it is when a child calls you by your first name.

It's been easier, and harder, to go through than around. There is no detour when it comes to ending a marriage. "You will have to walk through the fire," my therapist tells me, and she's right. Nobody does this for you. It's a grown-up thing, this divorce business.

You dig through the ashes for answers and realize that you are just as imperfect as you fear, that all those clichés about change are excruciatingly true. I don't blame him. I don't blame me. I don't even blame change. Maybe I'm fooling myself, but adapting a Zen approach to it all helps immensely.

I watch my former resentments as they pass me by. While I don't shake their hand, I don't wave goodbye to them either. I'm not there yet. I ache to be that evolved. Maybe I will be one day. There is frustration and anger that lie below any relationship; we are not special.

The single, burning stack of expectations falls as the pieces scrabble for new places to land.

I realize control is an illusion. We cannot shape a tattered love that's no longer there, yet I can choose to cherish joyful memories and be thankful for happy times and amazing kids. The idea that perhaps it's possible we've salvaged enough of this shredded relationship to still care about each other and our family makes me if not happy, at least grateful for this solo walk.

I'm damaged. I'm healing. I'm tending my scars.

The way it is with any kind of burn.

I Weep with Discovery

Is there one moment, one singular, clarifying *flash* out of the millions I've lived in this intricate, perplexing life, when I realized I owned my desire? There is, and it was transcendent.

Our minds are housed in rented homes we didn't choose. From a muffled peace thrust into a terrifying light, we are slammed with an onslaught of emotions that make no sense, with senses that create vexing emotions we cannot possibly understand.

Our outside wrappings appear vastly different, yet where do body and mind merge?

"Own your shit," we order people, and many of us do—we think. Yet how can we own that which we rent? We own it only to the extent we can comprehend it. How can an eleven-year-old girl understand the next-door neighbor who craves fondling her lithe young body at the same time he threatens her? Helping himself to her shell, to satisfy his own sick desires. To this day, I cannot comprehend that.

That's not my shit to own, though those memories have claimed their territory, rude houseguests who never leave.

Wandering through decades of callous objectification, my mind continuing to push the cerebral path, ignoring the anxious cries of my body. Once again, missing the clues of this merging of body and mind, not knowing how to recognize what had no name, thinking panic and depression were simply part of everyone's daily life.

Marriage, children, jobs, home … living the rote, "happy" life on paper, when in truth I dealt with an emotionally checked out partner, my faith crumbling in him—and in us—daily. I eventually began my search. A woman is more than a shell, and this woman longed to *feel* desire, to hunger and crave, and yes, to be craved and hungered for by a trusting, loving partner.

I sought a man who wouldn't objectify and use me. Not love, not lust, desire requires submission—something I'd fought, and run from, since age eleven.

The moment came with his warm eyes on mine, body protectively wrapped around me, his strong hands gently around me, claiming and owning me, and I gave myself to him. No games here, a total melding of vulnerability and passion, I submitted fully to desire, letting go completely for what was truly the first time.

I can't tell you where I went, but I can tell you it was instinctive, intuitive, primal. Owning this motherfucking body, my mind riding fire … so *in* it, I drowned.

A psychologist would likely explain that I lived most of my life in a fairly dissociative state, and I wouldn't disagree; a common coping technique for sexual assault survivors. It doesn't happen as much anymore, now that I'm in recovery and recognize when I drift (though I often recognized it as it happened, I didn't have a name for it). To me, everybody could look at themselves from the outside and observe. That was my normal.

Owning my body, finally, meant possessing and understanding desire while evaluating how to be present. Did I realize that I had, in a way, been denying how fully capable I could feel? Perhaps, in the same way one puts off spring cleaning or writing that term paper, dismissing the dangers of minimization.

Struggling with the puzzling contradiction of surrendering to empowerment makes my bewildered bones ache. How can I allow myself to enjoy *sublime pleasure* when that tiny nugget lingers … when didn't I get to decide?

Fear spreads covert tendrils throughout our souls, dropping seeds of shame along the way. The hardest battle I fought in unearthing my desire was the constant sway of overt sexuality. Even as I moved with confidence into warm skin and tousled sheets, that voice would command a surreptitious retreat.

Are you sure? Maybe you need a reason not to do this.

Swirling questions fill my mind, quaking my confidence.

Does owning our beauty, our sexuality, and the way it affects others, make us hollow?

If I admit to myself that sex can astonish, does that make me "a bad girl?"

Wearing the neon sign of "tainted by sexual abuse" already, how can—or must I—travel the path people stupidly refer to as "slut," when I'd spent years meticulously formulating the inadvertent good girl?

I caress permission like a lover in that instant. I am an adult woman who will no longer stifle the strength of my vulnerability. I make my own life choices, including when, how, and with whom I orgasm, desire, and ultimately love. I welcome the wild, messy child of the unknown, inviting her in to saturate my being.

I weep with the beauty of discovery.

The Mask of Congeniality

The divorce became final in December 2015, yet the relationship doesn't end, does it? You think it will, but it won't. You want it to be amicable, wearing your mask of congeniality while stabs of resentment surface, sizzling bubbles forming faster than you can slap them back down.

"Quiet," you whisper, "someone will hear," as if people hadn't noticed the tattered seams already.

It's all about stuff; things I don't even care about that I didn't even know I had. He wants it all. Fine, take it. A beach umbrella, a French press, the Disney blankets. Nothing expensive he can't replace but now he suddenly cannot live without and Must Have Right Away.

For his trip to Tomorrowland, apparently.

Nothing about the wrenching of lives is simple, no matter how much we desire it. He's moved on, I've moved on—all as it should be. Somehow, still, he's angry at me for wanting to be free of him. So that's my debt to be paid in full. With a new, higher, interest rate, added daily.

Life is so much bigger than tit for tat. Maybe I'm too close to know, to add a label to behaviors I don't understand and, frankly, don't have to care about anymore. As long as my kids are cared and provided for when they're with him, and returned to me when they need to be, my requirements of him are minimal.

All that's left now is The Money. The one thing that plagues most couples when they're together still stands before them with an ax to grind when they're not. Did you pay this? Will you pay for that?

I could choose to be angry, resentful, and upset—I've run through all those emotions, believe me—but now I choose resolution. I've always chosen resolution, but there are steps to grief—divorce is a death, you see. I tried to skip over those steppingstones of grief because I asked for the divorce. I thought I was special and could skip right over those hot coals. Nope. Turns out I'm no different than any other human whose been through this.

Dammit.

We are not matched on this rocky path, nor likely will we ever be.

Compassion sits me down and tells me he's struggling—with money, with anger, with control. He needs time to figure out how to sit with this new suit of armor, deflecting my readiness to make it easy on us all.

Frustration questions, "Why?"

Impatience snaps, "Dude, own your shit."

Exhaustion pushes me to the couch where I sleep and wake up fatigued because the emotional toll hasn't eased, anxiety poised for another snappish bomb headed my way.

Worry says, "I'm wasteful."

On goes my mask as I step around this emotional minefield, picking each word with thoughtful care. And what happens when I get to the other side? Is there even another side?

When I remove the mask occasionally, I breathe in cleansing air, relax, and focus on loving, writing, and work, grateful for the strength and support of loved ones, family, friends, and a good lawyer.

The process is long and not easy. And even when it is, it isn't.

Dust

Yesterday holds my anger in its palm.
The swirling red appears
flowing from your petty lies,
watching jagged justifications and
ragged delusions I cannot comprehend.

I simply ... flipped the switch—
from raging to calm
flowing water quelling my heart.
What you do no longer matters
in my forever unquiet mind.

Yesterday lasted many decades,
years of spinning time
placing outlandish tales so carefully on my waiting tongue—
anxious for one crystal sparkling truth ...
fool's gold.

I let it go.
I let you go.
All of it.

The writing mass falls away.
Gone.
Ashes to ashes.

Whatever remains you gather and throw
this dirt that I watch blow,
wind carrying away.
the sand of you falling ...
dust to dust.

Mercy House

Nobody's home at
the Mercy House.
His knocks,
his calls
his demands—
unanswered.
There is no grace for the Man of Lies.

The House breathed life through troubled walls
over two decades of painted love.
Belief in The Man's truth
laying her down on his exquisite bed of lavish stories.
Offering her soul, searing her to his side
stealing more than just her heart.

Blind to his stealth, Mercy could not see till
windows of faith broke open doors of grief,
escaping alone in the velvet night.
Looking back on their Dream
her haunted soul cries for the wasted time

No winner resides in a home of aching loss—
only emptiness where love once lived.

Closure

What about closure?

People assume writing about surviving sexual abuse provides some kind of catharsis or closure. I find this assumption amusing. Nothing changes the actual abuse experiences.

Closure is a nice, pretty box, tied up with a big, red bow. It's something people hand to you with white gloves and hushed voices. "Here, now that your abuser is {insert whatever you'd like here: in jail, dead, admitted they abused you}, you can have closure," they say as they slowly back out of the room.

How kind of people to tell us what we are to do with the most invasive sexual crimes some psycho perpetuated against us. As if a few years in jail will erase holding us down, ripping away our autonomy, burning this memory of pain a criminal has imprinted onto our very souls until we die.

"Clean-up on aisle nine, Mable. We've got another shattered box of Closure over here. And bring the Catharsis while you're at it!"

Closure is a way people tell survivors to get over it because they are uncomfortable with our pain. It's not out of malice; it's more of a way to remove the mess before the spill.

"It must feel cathartic to release all this pain," people say.

Catharsis is a release of repressed emotions. Does writing release trauma? Does it resolve what happened in the past?

Experiences are situations that happened. They are *not* emotions. Sure, we have attached emotions to those experiences, which are dizzyingly complicated and often feel like cumbersome boulders that will bury us. Sadly, for some they do.

Some hand us this trite little box of terms. "Here's your closure. Here's your catharsis. Would you like a side of forgiveness with that? You know, you'll heal much faster if you forgive your abuser, right? Or at least forgive yourself."

Healing from abuse—abuse recovery, whatever you choose to call it—is a survivor's right. We don't walk this path alone, though it often feels like it. We deserve whatever type of support we need. If it's helpful to an individual to refer to it as closure, catharsis, or forgiveness, cool. Their choice.

My point is: Don't assume anything about a survivor, except we need, and have every right to ask for, compassion and support.

How Abuse Exhausts You

It's exhausting. The abuse.

He wasn't like this when we married. This overt, standing-over-me, red-in-the-face, pointing-fingers-and-yelling kind of abuse he does now. In front of other people, even. In front of our lawyers.

"Wow, he's out there, isn't he?" my lawyer says to me after such a display.

His own lawyer had to tell him, "Don't yell. Don't point," in one of those stark-white little meeting rooms that are barely comfortable for two. It's claustrophobic for four who are at odds.

I shake my head. "After all this time dealing with him, I can only interpret his behavior this way: His delusions are real to him. This is what happens when you call him out with facts," I reply.

I divorced him after twenty-two years and two children who live with me now (my fourteen-year-old son visits him occasionally). He doesn't pay a dime to help our daughter who is in her twenties (and anxious, OCD-stricken with therapy), her college, her car, or any kind of life stuff, and by law, he doesn't have to. He could choose to, yet he chooses not to, which crushes her.

That's on him.

I choose to care for her well-being and help her navigate adulthood, first jobs, and the myriad of forms that scholarships, financial aid, student loans, and grants require. And I pay for whatever she needs to the extent that I'm able. He calls her once in a while to see if she's seen the latest Marvel movie or whatever other common ground he can find.

He visits for a day, and she watches him give $20 to my son. None for her.

"Make your own money, honey," she tells me he tells her.

My son tells me he doesn't know what to do with the money. "It feels dirty and sad now."

My children are too young to feel this. To know this.

It's exhausting. The abuse.

She wavers in taking his calls. "He's like that bad boyfriend who keeps breaking my heart, except he's my father which makes it even worse," she says, her big, hazel eyes shiny with tears. She never expected her first heartbreak to come from someone to whom she's biologically related. She doesn't want to be the girl with "daddy issues."

"What a fucking cliché," she adds.

"Why am I the one who has to suffer because of his fuck-ups?" she asks me.*

Probably a question all children of divorce ask their parents.

"I don't know how to answer, baby."

Probably the answer all parents of divorce tell their children, the real answer pregnant with bitterness that need not be birthed right now.

I put off divorce for a long time because I wanted to avoid this exact kind of hurt. This exact kind of abusive bullshit.

We always said—promised—we'd put the kids' needs first if we ever split. The promises of smug marrieds.

This is only the microscopic tip of what's happened in the years since the divorce. I don't share much because it's a map of convoluted toxicity, and to be honest, it's terrifying. I have accusatory email trails that could reach the moon. Why write about it?

Well, writers write. I've chosen not to share previously because it's nobody's damn business, yet also out of fear. The few pieces I did

write, he read and tried to use against me as some kind of ammuni-
tion that I'm, let's see … a "man-hating feminist who hates men"
(hilarious for so many reasons, I know).

My attorney: "Um, she lives with a guy. You know that, right?"

My loving, supportive dad and sweet brother-in-law came to
court to support this "man-hating feminist."

My heart filled with very un-feminist-like pink cupcake frosting
that day.

I spent over twenty years with a man who constantly interrupted
me, talked over me, didn't want me to discuss that I was a survivor of
childhood sexual abuse (especially with our kids), and financially
abused me. Not to mention the gaslighting and emotional abuse
which still triggers me in ways I don't even realize or understand until
my heart jumps like a bunny when I see a new email from him,
bracing myself to deal with more.

That unidentifiable, all-encompassing, fatiguing "more."

Such an odd land for this survivor to be in, especially since I
didn't buy a ticket to travel here, so I decided the rules had to change.
I choose to have as little interaction with him as possible. I've blocked
him everywhere, including my phone, save email.

Will I leave this foreign land stronger? You bet. That's also why
I'm sharing now. Finally. I'm not hiding how difficult this all is. I'm
sure he sees things very differently. Do I care? No. I can't control his
feelings or perceptions, and bothering is a waste of time and effort.

Why didn't I leave sooner? Isn't that the question everyone asks
of an abused woman? (Abused? Something he'd scoff at, surely.) I
hate that question. It's nobody's damn business. However, in my most
embarrassing truth, in my most vulnerable moments, I ask myself
this question a lot.

I didn't realize most of it was happening. There it is. My
truth. When you're in it, you don't see it. I honestly had no idea.
Emotional and financial abuse are insidious. It's not like he hit me
and left bruises or broken bones. He left doubts. He left questions. He
left massive debts. That's all detritus I'm still working through now.

The abuse.

It's exhausting.

*My adult daughter gave me full permission to share her mental health issues and thoughts about her father for this piece. She wants other kids of divorce to know what it's like (her words).

DOUBT

I breathe doubt like dust.

Bombarding me
With tiny bits of ash
She's there
Alive, awake
In me
Floating by with her knowing smile

I slap her away
And finally, truly catch a deep, cleansing breath.

Yet she's back with a trace
The slightest layering
Blowing away my calm
With a flick of a transparent finger.

Why doesn't she let me free?

I breathe you in
I won't let her pull you from my bones.

I want you.
I want us.

Surely, one pure breath is enough?

I see our truth flowing
The everything of
Wanting
Wondering
In your eyes.

If only doubt would float away
Then breath would be so easy
And so, would we.

Additional Reading

Writing about my experiences as a survivor has helped others understand they are not alone. Connecting with professionals who study and treat survivors daily is incredibly eye-opening, so I want to share six articles and studies which will help you, survivor friends, understand why you feel what you feel.

I know I'm on the right path because rape culture, ignorance, and cruelty still exist. I don't know why people spew venom on sexual abuse survivors when we did nothing wrong, but they do—which is not our problem. However, we can educate and arm ourselves with scientific data on how trauma affects us.

So, the next time you run across Dodgeball Dude or I-Don't-Get-Trauma Girl, please send them one of these articles.

HOW CHILDHOOD TRAUMA AFFECTS HEALTH ACROSS A LIFETIME, TEDTALK[1]

"Childhood trauma isn't something you just get over as you grow up. Pediatrician Nadine Burke Harris explains that the repeated stress of abuse, neglect and parents struggling with mental health or substance abuse issues has real, tangible effects on the development of the brain. This unfolds across a lifetime, to the point where those who've experienced high levels of trauma are at triple the risk for heart disease and lung cancer. An impassioned plea for pediatric medicine to confront the prevention and treatment of trauma, head-on."

Nadine Burke Harris, Pediatrician

ACES STUDY [2]

The CDC-Kaiser Permanente Adverse Childhood Experiences (ACE) Study is one of the largest investigations of childhood abuse and neglect and later-life health and well-being.

The original ACE Study was conducted at Kaiser Permanente from 1995 to 1997 with two waves of data collection. Over 17,000 Health Maintenance Organization members from Southern California receiving physical exams completed confidential surveys regarding their childhood experiences and current health status and behaviors.

The CDC continues ongoing surveillance of ACEs by assessing the medical status of the study participants via periodic updates of morbidity and mortality data.

More detailed information about the study can be found in the links below or in "Relationship of Childhood Abuse and Household Dysfunction to Many of the Leading Causes of Death in Adults,"[3] published in the American Journal of Preventive Medicine.

There is *so* much information here. Start with the basic assessment, then move on to what it means. In particular, you can learn more how survivors are prone to these disease states and why (I was particularly interested in headaches, as I've suffered from debilitating migraines since my teens).

PTSD

Post-Traumatic Stress Disorder is a psychiatric disorder that can occur following the experience or witnessing of a life-threatening event such as military combat, natural disasters, terrorist incidents, serious accidents, or physical or sexual assault in adult or childhood. You can read more about the symptoms of PTSD and what to look for at the U.S. Department of Veteran Affairs.[4]

The study, *Traumatic Stress: Effects on the Brain,* [5] is particularly enlightening, By breaking down what happens to each section of the brain (referenced in Dr. Burke Harris' TEDTalk above), you get a much better idea of why survivors behave and react the way we do. As I say when I share this chart, "This is your brain on PTSD."

It's important to note the incidence of PTSD is higher in survivors of rape, CSA, and sexual assault than other types of trauma.

• 94% of women who are raped experience symptoms of post-traumatic stress disorder (PTSD) during the two weeks following the rape.

• 30% of women report symptoms of PTSD 9 months after the rape.

• 33% of women who are raped contemplate suicide.

• 13% of women who are raped attempt suicide.

• Approximately 70% of rape or sexual assault victims experience moderate to severe distress, a larger percentage than for any other violent crime. (Source: RAINN) [6]

"Life After Rape" by Carrie Arnold: WOMEN'S HEALTH MAGAZINE [7]

"PTSD typically takes the form of nightmares, flashbacks, and feelings of guilt and shame that can surface right away or years after a trauma. But it can also manifest in physical ways, like chronic pain, intestinal problems, muscle cramps, or, even paralyzed vocal cords. For 94 percent of survivors, symptoms last at least two weeks; for a full half of them, they persist for years, even decades—sometimes long after the victim thinks she has laid the ghosts to rest.

Consider the women, some now in their sixties, still grappling with the effects of decades-old alleged assaults by comedian Bill Cosby. German researchers found a third of women raped during World War II had PTSD symptoms nearly 70 years later."

BOYS AND GIRLS ARE AFFECTED DIFFERENTLY [8]

Traumatic stress affects the brains of adolescent boys and girls differently, according to a new brain-scanning study from the Stanford University School of Medicine.

Among youth with post-traumatic stress disorder, the study found structural differences between the sexes in one part of the insula, a brain region that detects cues from the body and processes emotions and empathy. The insula helps to integrate one's feelings, actions and several other brain functions. The study is the first to show differences between male and female PTSD patients in a part of the insula involved in emotion and empathy.

ABUSE AND HOW IT AFFECTS DNA [9]

Does this sound like science fiction to you? Well, it's not.

"Recent evidence from molecular studies has shown that
telomere length—a measure of cellular aging—is strongly
influenced by a broad spectrum of stress. Telomere erosion
might be accelerated by traumatic stress, and traumatic stress
has shown to be associated with the risk of developing
chronic diseases like cancer, cardiovascular diseases, and
immunologic conditions." (Journal of Trauma and
Treatment)

Not only does abuse affect the survivor's DNA (telomeres, to be specific), but it can also affect future generations!

Pretty mind-blowing stuff. The link above is really scientific and not light reading, I'll warn you right now. But I feel it's important to include because it's a new and fascinating area of study.

---

1. Harris, Nadine Burke, MD. "How Childhood Trauma Affects Health across a Lifetime." TEDMED. September 2014. Accessed September 06, 2018. https://tedmed.com/talks/show?id=293066.
2. "Violence Prevention." Centers for Disease Control and Prevention. April 01, 2016. Accessed September 06, 2018. https://www.cdc.gov/violenceprevention/acestudy/journal.html.
3. Felitti, Vincent J., MD, FACP, Robert F. Anda, MD, MS, Dale Nordenberg, MD, David F. Williamson, MS, PhD, Alison M. Spitz, MS, MPH, Valerie Edwards, BA, Mary P. Koss, PhD, and James S. Marks, MD, MPH. "Relationship of Childhood Abuse and Household Dysfunction to Many of the Leading Causes of Death in Adults." American Journal of Preventive Medicine 14, no. 4 (May 1998): 245-58. doi:https://doi.org/10.1016/S0749-3797(98)00017-8.

4. National Center. "PTSD: National Center for PTSD." Negative Coping and PTSD - PTSD: National Center for PTSD. August 15, 2013. Accessed September 06, 2018. https://www.ptsd.va.gov/.

5. Bremner, J Douglas. "Traumatic Stress: Effects on the Brain." Dialogues in clinical neuroscience. Les Laboratoires Servier, December 2006. https://www.ncbi.nlm.nih.gov/pmc/articles/PMC3181836/.

6. "Victims of Sexual Violence: Statistics | RAINN." Adult Survivors of Child Sexual Abuse | RAINN. Accessed September 06, 2018. https://www.rainn.org/statistics/victims-sexual-violence.

7. Arnold, Carrie. "Life After Rape: The Sexual Assault Issue No One's Talking About." Women's Health. May 25, 2018. Accessed September 06, 2018. https://www.womenshealthmag.com/life/a19899018/ptsd-after-rape/.

8. Digitale, Erin. "Traumatic Stress Changes Brains of Boys, Girls Differently." Stanford Medicine News Center. November 11, 2016. Accessed September 06, 2018. https://med.stanford.edu/news/all-news/2016/11/traumatic-stress-changes-brains-of-boys-girls-differently.html.

9. Küffer, A., A. Maercker, and A. Burri. "Transgenerational Effects of PTSD or Traumatic Stress: Do Telomeres Reach Across the Generations?" Journal of Trauma & Treatment 3, no. 3, 1-8. Accessed July 28, 2014. doi:10.4172/2167-1222.1000204.

Work Cited

Arnold, Carrie. "Life After Rape: The Sexual Assault Issue No One's Talking About." Women's Health. May 25, 2018. Accessed September 06, 2018. https://www.womenshealthmag.com/life/a19899018/ptsd-after-rape/.

Capote, Truman. Breakfast at Tiffany's and Three Stories. Saint Joseph, MO: Rolling Hills Consolidated Library, 2015.

Digitale, Erin. "Traumatic Stress Changes Brains of Boys, Girls Differently." Stanford Medicine News Center. November 11, 2016. Accessed September 06, 2018. https://med.stanford.edu/news/all-news/2016/11/traumatic-stress-changes-brains-of-boys-girls-differently.html.

Felitti, Vincent J., MD, FACP, Robert F. Anda, MD, MS, Dale Nordenberg, MD, David F. Williamson, MS, PhD, Alison M. Spitz, MS, MPH, Valerie Edwards, BA, Mary P. Koss, PhD, and James S. Marks, MD, MPH. "Relationship of Childhood Abuse and Household Dysfunction to Many of the Leading Causes of Death in Adults." *American Journal of Preventive Medicine* 14, no. 4 (May 1998): 245-58. doi: https://doi.org/10.1016/S0749-3797(98)00017-8.

Harris, Nadine Burke, MD. "How Childhood Trauma Affects Health across a Lifetime." TEDMED. September 2014. Accessed September 06, 2018. https://tedmed.com/talks/show?id=293066.

Küffer, A., A. Maercker, and A. Burri. "Transgenerational Effects of PTSD or Traumatic Stress: Do Telomeres Reach Across the Generations?" *Journal of Trauma & Treatment*3, no. 3, 1-8. Accessed July 28, 2014. doi:10.4172/2167-1222.1000204.

National Center. "PTSD: National Center for PTSD." Negative Coping and PTSD - PTSD: National Center for PTSD. August 15, 2013. Accessed September 06, 2018. https://www.ptsd.va.gov/.

"Victims of Sexual Violence: Statistics | RAINN." Adult Survivors of Child Sexual Abuse | RAINN. Accessed September 06, 2018. https://www.rainn.org/statistics/victims-sexual-violence.

"Violence Prevention." Centers for Disease Control and Prevention. April 01, 2016. Accessed September 06, 2018. https://www.cdc.gov/violenceprevention/acestudy/journal.html.

About the Author

As of 2021, Rachel is the author of 7 books, including the ***BadRedhead Media 30-Day Book Marketing Challenge***, which has successfully reached the Top 10 on Amazon's Business Writing List and has stayed on three Top 100 lists since its release, as well as winning multiple awards!

She is releasing her third and final BROKEN book, ***Broken People****, in Fall, 2021. She's also making all three BROKEN books available in an omnibus edition. Stay tuned for more info!*

Her first book **A *Walk In The Snark*** hit #1 on the Kindle Motherhood list in September 2011 (do you think they know she talks about sex? Shhh). She released ***The Mancode: Exposed*** right after Thanksgiving 2011 and by January, it placed in the Amazon Top 100 Paid!

Her third book, ***Broken Pieces***, is completely different in tone. While still non-fiction, it's not humor at all. She released it Christmas 2012, and it reached #1 on *Women's Studies and Gender Studies* within two weeks. She released her fourth book in 2015, ***Broken Places***, where it immediately hit #1 on several Amazon lists and has gone on to win several prestigious awards (see below).

Reviews and Awards

In March 2013, **The Midwest Book Review** gave *Broken Pieces* five stars, as did two Top 10 Hall of Fame Amazon reviewers. Summer 2013, *Broken Pieces* won best nonfiction honorable mention from the *San Francisco Book Festival*, best nonfiction and women's studies from the Global eBook Awards and eFestival of books among other awards. In Winter 2013 *Broken Pieces* hit #1 on

Amazon's Women's Poetry list and continues to rank highly in other Amazon categories.

Rachel released her fourth book, **_Broken Places_**, in January 2015. Within one week, her latest release reached the Top Five in Women's Poetry and #1 on Amazon's Hot Releases List. She won **First Place** in the **2017 Chanticleer Journey Awards for Narrative Non-Fiction!** and Honorable Mentions from both the San Francisco Book Festival in May 2015 as well as the Los Angeles Book Festival in Memoir and Non-Fiction.

She courageously confronts the topics of sexual abuse and suicide, love, and healing, in her second nonfiction book of prose and poetry (her fourth book overall). Rachel bares her soul in essays, poems, and prose, addressing life's most difficult topics with honesty. As you follow one woman's journey through the dark and into the light, you will find yourself forever changed.

"A talented writer with a journalism degree, Thompson adeptly plays with point of view employing both first person singular ("I") to convey her experiences, and first-person plural ("We"), perhaps to denote a kinship among survivors."

– Chanticleer Book Reviews

***

'A stellar achievement,'

~ Tracy Riva (Top Amazon Reviewer, Tracy Riva Reviews)

In 2011, Rachel founded **BadRedheadMedia** where she works with authors teaching social media, branding, and marketing (skills acquired through eighteen years of successful, award-winning Big Pharma marketing and sales). Connect with her at **BadRedhead-Media.com** for more about her company. Her articles appear regularly in **_The Huffington Post, Feminine Collective, Indie Reader, Medium, OnMogul, Blue Ink Review,_** and several others.

Writing Projects

Rachel is the founder and creator of #MondayBlogs, #BookMarketingChat, and #NaNoProMo (each May)- all completely free, writer-based phenomenons designed to help writers grow their author platforms, and learn how to market their books!

Advocacy

Connecting with other survivors of childhood sexual abuse and providing a safe place to discuss our stories has become an unexpected yet vital part of her own recovery. In addition to creating #SexAbuseChat on Twitter (every Tuesday, 6pm pst), Rachel created a secret Facebook group for adult survivors of childhood sexual abuse and is humbled to share many of her fellow authors' stories on her blog.

In 2016, Rachel teamed up with Dr. Shruti Kapoor to start **Speak Our Stories**, a blog and social media platform that combines their own advocacy platforms (Sayfty.com and Sex Abuse Chat) to give other survivors the opportunity to use their voice. Each survivor's stories is shared across social media, as well as on Medium, Mogul, and Huffington Post. To read these amazing survivor stories or submit your own, **find out more here.**

She's been on Twitter since 2009 and finds it a wonderful, fascinating platform to connect with readers, establish a fan base, and gain terrific connections, and create long-lasting relationships. In October 2012, Rachel and her family moved north to Northern California, closer to family and friends. Well, that and because her family was tired of her burnt food and Rachel's mom is a great cook. In 2013, *Broken Pieces* was released for the first time in print, an accomplishment Rachel is very proud of.

In today's world of book sales, all authors need book reviews from readers posted to the various online retailers. Since you picked up one of my books, you might be an author - a writer. I encourage you to post an honest review of this book, when you are finished, to the retail site you purchased it from. This action you will help you experience what you will ask your readers to do. It is easier to ask this of your readers if you understand the process.

Thank you so much!

Other Books

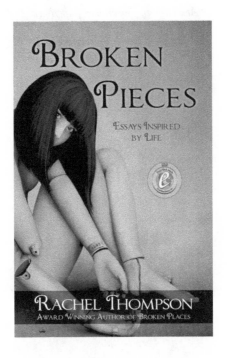

Broken Pieces
https://geni.us/Broken_Pieces
Available in e-book and paperback

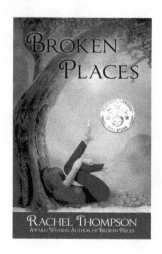

Broken Places
https://geni.us/BrokenPlaces
Available in e-book and paperback

The BadRedhead Media 30-Day Book Marketing Challenge
https://geni.us/30DayMarketing
Available in e-book and paperback

BadRedhead Media: How to Best Optimize Blog Posts for SEO: 25 Tested Tips
Writers Need to Know Now
https://geni.us/BlogPostsSEO
Available in e-book

Anthologies:

Love Notes From Humanity: The Lust, Love & Loss Collection
https://geni.us/LoveNotesP
Available in e-book and paperback

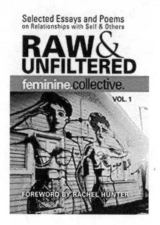

*Feminine Collective: Raw and Unfiltered Vol 1: Selected Essays and Poems on
Relationships with Self and Others*
https://geni.us/RawUnfilteredP
Available in e-book and paperback